Original title:
Bamboo Ballads

Copyright © 2025 Creative Arts Management OÜ
All rights reserved.

Author: Robert Ashford
ISBN HARDBACK: 978-1-80566-645-5
ISBN PAPERBACK: 978-1-80566-930-2

The Spiritual Whispers of the Wild

In the forest where giggles grow,
Trees sway and dance to a show.
Critters convene with hats on their heads,
While squirrels sip tea in their cozy beds.

A raccoon in boots prances with flair,
A bear doing cartwheels, oh what a pair!
Owl wears glasses, reading the news,
While rabbits in tuxedos twirl in their shoes.

The brook plays music, a splash and a plop,
Frogs leap like dancers, they never stop.
The wind tells secrets in whispers so bright,
As the moon chuckles softly, lighting the night.

From shadows, the fox plays a prank or two,
Stealing hats from the deer, oh who knew?
Laughter echoes beneath the tall trees,
As nature embraces its wild, funny tease.

Dance of the Tall Silhouettes

In the wind they weave and sway,
Tall silhouettes in bright array.
They giggle and wiggle, oh what a sight,
Dancing with glee under the moonlight.

Their leaves are clapping, a clever cheer,
Eager to show off, they've nothing to fear.
With every twist, they tease the breeze,
A joyful performance with such ease.

Songs of the Rustic Stalks

Rustic stalks with voices so bright,
They sing and chirp from morning to night.
Their melody tickles, a merry refrain,
Riding the rhythm of a soft summer rain.

A hiccup, a giggle, a joyful shout,
Echoes of laughter, swirling about.
In harmony, they sway without care,
Creating a ruckus in the open air.

Murmurs of the Verdant Breeze

Whispers of green, they tell a tale,
Of pranks and games in the softest gale.
A rustle here and a rustle there,
Mischievous breezes dance everywhere.

They poke and tease, a playful tease,
Scoffing at clouds with the greatest of ease.
A giggle escapes from the rustling leaves,
As the wind spins stories that no one believes.

The Lullaby of Swaying Shoots

Swaying shoots with a lullaby tune,
Crooning gently beneath the moon.
Each stroke a caress, a wink, a sigh,
Lulling the critters that drift on by.

While crickets pitch in with their own song,
They jive with the rhythm, a life all along.
As stars twinkle down with a lighthearted glow,
The night holds a humor only they know.

Rhythm of the Rustling Leaves

In a dance of green, they sway,
Tickling the breeze in a playful way.
They gossip and laugh with the wind,
Each secret a giggle, never pinned.

The sunlight twinkles on their attire,
As they flirt with clouds, never tire.
A rustle sounds like a wacky tune,
Nature's own band, beneath the moon.

Serenity in the Stalks

In the stalks, the critters play,
Chasing shadows, come what may.
A squirrel spins tales of daring feats,
While a frog croaks favorite beats.

The grasshoppers tap their tiny shoes,
With antics that give us all the blues.
A calm that's funny, a silly trance,
Nature throws its outrageous dance.

Where the Swaying Sweetness Lies

Beneath the sway, the sweets do hide,
With honeyed whispers, they serve and bide.
Bees burst with laughter, buzzing cheer,
As sugar crumbs spread far and near.

The roots shake hands with the grass so tall,
In a giggling game of catch and ball.
Each sapling grins, a cheeky sprite,
In this sunny patch, delight takes flight.

Melodies from the Verdant Veil

In the veil where the soft moss lies,
The chirping sounds make you theorize.
A symphony played by creatures small,
They strut and sway; they've got no sprawl.

The wind hums low, a breezy jest,
As lizards bask in their leafy fest.
Nature's pratfall, a sight to see,
In a world where giggles roam free.

Dreams Among the Towering Greens

In a forest where tall stalks sway,
A squirrel sings in a curious way.
Tickling the leaves with a gentle strum,
"Dance with me, come have some fun!"

The raccoon giggles, scratching its head,
"I'd rather nap here in my bed."
While a frog croaks out a silly tune,
"Let's send our dreams to the moon!"

The Enigmatic Harmony of Leaves

Underneath the green canopy's cheer,
A chattering parrot is drawing near.
"Why don't trees wear shoes and hats?"
He questions, while balancing on the mats.

The leaves respond with a rustle and sway,
"Because we're stylish in our own way!"
Their laughter mingles with the breeze,
"Wear a leaf crown, if you please!"

The Lyrical Dance of Nature's Giants

Giant stalks twist in a jovial prance,
Inviting all critters to join the dance.
An owl hoots in rhythm, "Let's groove!"
As ants march proudly, feeling the move.

A turtle joins in, slow but bright,
Swaying his shell to the left and right.
"Who knew we could dance so free?"
Echoes through the canopy with glee.

The Soundtrack of Quiet Reflections

In the shade, a whisper floats,
Telling tales of old jokes and gloat.
A beetle rolls its laughter wide,
While mushrooms chuckle side by side.

"Why did the leaf blush?" asked a vine,
"Because the breeze said, 'You're so fine!'"
Their giggles ripple, a joyful sound,
In this merry green kingdom, bliss is found.

The Language of the Leaves

In the breeze they chime and sway,
Leaves gossip secrets gained each day.
Ticklish branches tickle the sun,
While squirrels hold a comedy run.

A leaf's chuckle floats through the air,
As a snail claims it's a grand affair.
To dance with joy, a twig does spin,
While the grass grins wide with a cheeky grin.

Songs of the Verdant Whisper.

Branches lean in, sharing a jest,
With roots deep down, oh what a fest!
The flowers giggle, teasing the moon,
While frogs croak tunes in a silly tune.

A playful breeze hums through the wood,
Spreading loud laughter, oh how it should!
A wobbling leaf trips on its fate,
Then winks at the ground, feeling first-rate.

Whispers of the Green Grove

In the pockets of shade, jokes are found,
As acorns tease the ground all around.
A grinning trunk tells tales of old,
While daisies dance in fine hats of gold.

The shadows join in with silly grace,
Tickling the toad with a playful face.
They roll with laughter, no one's too shy,
As the sun peeks in with a twinkling eye.

Echoes in the Forest Canopy

Echoes bounce through the leafy dome,
As owls swap jokes in their nighttime home.
A chipmunk freestyles with vibrant flair,
While the stars giggle, without a care.

They ponder how leaves wear hats so grand,
And whether the wind is in high demand.
In this laughter above, spirits unite,
As the night serenades all with delight.

The Allure of the Swaying Stalks

In the breeze, they dance and twirl,
Sticks in a line, oh what a whirl!
Giggling leaves, a jovial sound,
Nature's jesters, laughter unbound.

A critter hops, trying to prance,
Between the stalks, it takes a chance.
But whoops, it trips and starts to roll,
A comical tumble, it's on a stroll.

The shade a cool, whimsical embrace,
As the sun flicks paint on their face.
With every sway, there comes a cheer,
The forest chuckles, it's all quite clear.

Oh, how they shake on a windy day,
Like a band of fools in a playful fray.
Join the frolic, let worries flee,
In the sway of the stalks, we're all so free!

The Gentle Cadence of Earth

When the ground hums with a gentle tune,
Earthworms wiggle, making us swoon.
A jig from the roots, a tap from the leaves,
Laughter sprouts up from underground weaves.

The insects buzz like a silly band,
With tiny legs tap-dancing on sand.
The sun peeks in with a bright, cheeky grin,
As critters gather, let the fun begin!

A squirrel with style, wearing a hat,
In a dance-off, oh, what a spat!
He twirls and spins, trying to boast,
While the leaves clap, like a lively host.

Nature's rhythm brings giggles anew,
Step to the beat, let your wild side brew.
In this earthy lounge, let joy take you far,
Dance with the critters, beneath the gold star!

The Serene Echo of Nature's Chorus

Listen close, there's laughter around,
In the whispers of leaves, joy can be found.
A chorus of giggles, a playful joke,
As the flowers nod, they too want to poke.

A frog croaks low, it's offbeat and fun,
While the crickets chirp, they're never outdone.
They throw a bash, oh what a sight,
With nature's night band, the mood is just right.

The fireflies flicker, like stars on the ground,
Doing the dance where silliness abounds.
Join in the rhythm, let laughter take flight,
In the echo of nature, the world's feeling right.

As the dusk rolls in, the fun isn't done,
Under the moon, take a spin and run.
So gather your friends, and find your delight,
In this serene chorus, let's party all night!

The Ballads of Sun-Kissed Canes

Sun-kissed canes sway with glee,
Bouncing around like kids at a spree.
They tip and they tilt, what a funny sight,
Chasing each other in the warm sunlight.

A grasshopper leaps, then gives it a go,
In a tap dance battle, don't you know?
The canes chuckle, they can't keep still,
As the grasshoppers show off their skill.

When the wind whispers secrets so sweet,
The canes do a twist – oh, ain't that neat!
With giggles galore, they share all the jokes,
Laughing along with the playful folks.

Come one, come all, join the game's cheer,
The sun-kissed canes are spreading good cheer.
In a world filled with dance, where troubles fade,
Let the laughter roll on, we've got it made!

Secrets of the Verdant Thicket

In the thicket, whispers play,
Secrets dance in a leafy sway.
Frogs in tuxedos, singing loud,
While crickets cheer, a lively crowd.

A raccoon steals a shiny spoon,
While vines giggle beneath the moon.
Squirrels hold a nutty feast,
As owls hoot, they're quite the beast.

A mouse in boots plays the flute,
And ants march by in a little suit.
Laughter echoes through the trees,
A symphony of joyous ease.

So if you wander, stop and peek,
The thicket holds a cheeky streak.
With jests and jesters on the ground,
In this green world, fun is found.

Ode to the Flexible Giants

Oh, flexible giants, bending low,
Knocking hats off folks below.
Each sway a prank, a gentle tease,
With giggles carried on the breeze.

In summer sun, they sway and sway,
Tickling noses in a cheeky play.
Birds atop are quick to jest,
"Hold on tight, lest you be pressed!"

They catch the wind, a rustling sound,
With branches dancing all around.
In every twist, a story spun,
Laughter shared is never done.

So raise a cheer, and lift your cup,
For giants here just can't stop up.
With their charm, the world feels bright,
In the stretch of day, all's delight.

Verses Beneath the Swirling Canopy

Underneath the leafy sky,
Whispers of the breeze go by.
A parrot tells a joke or two,
While lizards laugh in vibrant hue.

With jolly frogs in little hats,
They plan a dance with furry rats.
Each step a tumble, a joyful fall,
As laughter rises, bounces, calls.

The canopy swirls, a lively stage,
Where nature's humor takes the page.
A squirrel juggles acorns in twos,
While the ants host a game of snooze.

So join the fun beneath the leaves,
Where mirth appears and never grieves.
With every twist and turn, you'll find,
The joy of nature is intertwined.

The Sonnet of Shimmering Leaves

Oh, shimmering leaves in the bright sun's glare,
   They twirl and spin like dancers in glee.
   In the laughter of breezes, a playful air,
Where nature's wittiness flows wild and free.

   A squirrel thinks he's a ninja quite bold,
Leaps from a branch with a thud and a cheer.
   While in the shadows, secrets unfold,
   As wise owls chuckle, gathering near.

Each rustle and whisper a punchline concealed,
 A punchy remark from the grasshopper friend.
   In the theater of leaves, joy is revealed,
Where merriment echoes and never will end.

So here's to the wonder in nature's embrace,
  With shimmering leaves, we find our place.

Songs of the Verdant Pathways

In the forest, sticks do dance,
Chasing shadows, what a prance!
Squirrels wear their fanciest hats,
While frogs debate with chatty bats.

Leaves are laughing, roots are grooving,
As the little bugs start moving.
With every rustle, giggles flare,
The trees join in, beyond compare!

Grasshoppers on a tango spree,
Jumping high, oh so carefree!
A parade of twigs and clovers,
Nature's humor never hovers.

Whispering winds blow through the glade,
Tickling leaves as jokes are played.
In this green, a clownish crew,
Where joy is found in every view.

Flute of the Forest Heart

A squirrel plays a wooden flute,
As rabbits dance, oh what a hoot!
The mushrooms nod, with caps so bright,
To the jolly tunes that spark the night.

Crickets join with chirps so loud,
In perfect sync, they form a crowd.
The nocturnal choir fills the air,
As nightingales fluff their pretty hair.

The owls roll eyes at silly jests,
As fireflies wear their glowing vests.
Each note a giggle, wild and free,
In leafy halls of harmony.

Twirling ferns, with wavy grace,
Join in the nightly music chase.
A concert of whimsy and cheer,
In the forest, the fun is near.

Cadence of the Green Symphony

The whispering leaves start a chat,
Inviting all from butterfly to brat.
Dancing shadows, with mischief they play,
Nature's orchestra, come what may!

The worms form bands beneath the ground,
Creating rhythms, oh so profound!
The snails sashay, a slow parade,
Proudly flaunting their shimmering shade.

The ants march on in quirky lines,
With tiny hats and clever designs.
Their tiny tunes, a joyful din,
With every step, a giggle within.

Breezes whistle a cheeky tune,
As tadpoles sway under the moon.
In this green wonder, a comical show,
Where laughter sprouts and hearts will glow.

Nature's Unseen Serenade

Whimsical whispers rustle near,
As crickets sing of silly fear.
The owls hoot with cheeky glee,
What mysteries hide in that tall tree?

A family of frogs, dressed in plaid,
Debating which one is the 'most rad.'
While peeking hedgehogs try to hear,
Their giggles echo, far and near.

Vines hang low like a playful tease,
Inviting creatures to dance with ease.
The melody of nature spins tight,
In this wild revelry of delight.

With every bloom, a joke unfolds,
As daisies tease the marigolds.
A hidden world of laughter waits,
In nature's arms, hilarity creates.

Verses in the Whispering Wood

In the woods where whispers play,
The squirrels dance, come what may.
A rabbit hops, a fox takes flight,
While trees giggle, oh what a sight!

Beneath the shade of leaf and bough,
Frogs croak jokes; they don't know how.
The owls chuckle in the night,
As fireflies twinkle, just for spite.

With acorns rolling, what a mess!
The raccoons argue, who's the best?
Through laughter spills the soft moon glow,
Nature's humor steals the show!

In this realm where fun prevails,
A woodpecker tells the tallest tales.
With every bark, a punchline grows,
In the wood where laughter flows!

Breathing in the Earth's Chorus

The flowers sway with laughter bright,
As bees hum tunes from day to night.
A snail slides in with style and grace,
While crickets tap their own two-step pace.

The grasshoppers leap, they're quite the crew,
They jump so high, they play peek-a-boo!
With every breeze, the tunes combine,
Nature's band is simply divine!

A playful fox darts through the green,
Making friends with the unseen.
Their giggles echo, sweet and true,
In this chorus, hearts renew.

Leaves rustle, gossip flies like a kite,
And mushrooms chuckle at their own height.
Together they sing, without a care,
A symphony born from love and flair!

Raindrops on the Green Canopy

Raindrops shimmy, they twist and glide,
On leaves that giggle, tails held wide.
A puddle splashes, what a fun splash!
Dancing droplets make quite the dash!

The frogs lift their voices, bold and loud,
Telling tales to the smallest crowd.
While worms wiggle in the joyful mud,
Chasing dreams with a playful thud.

The wind joins in, a jester sly,
Tickling branches as it passes by.
Each droplet falls like a playful tease,
Creating laughter among the trees.

As rain forgets it's time to leave,
Mushrooms pop up, too much to believe!
In this wet wonder, joy does bloom,
Nature's punchline clears all gloom!

Serenade of Nature's Spine

The mountain hums a hearty tune,
With echoes bouncing, morning to moon.
A raccoon strums on a twiggy line,
Each note a wink, a twist, a sign.

The rivers laugh, they swirl and sway,
Telling secrets along the way.
With every pebble, a story flows,
In this serenade, anything goes!

Birds chirp in chorus, quite the surprise,
While the sun grins through velvety skies.
Each branch sways to a rhythm so fine,
In the groove of nature's spine.

As stars twinkle, the night takes flight,
Jokes hang heavy in the cool twilight.
In this concert of dusk and dawn,
The show goes on, forever drawn!

Sonnet of the Woodland Watchers

In the woods where the tall trees sway,
Squirrels dance in their nutty ballet.
Birds gossip like school kids at play,
While bugs wear hats, or so they say.

Rabbits hop in a game of tag,
With turtles who just laugh and brag.
The fox plays tricks, but can't catch a mag,
While chipmunks cheer, and the owl just smags.

The deer prance by in their Sunday best,
While raccoons plan their next big quest.
Amidst their laughter, we all feel blessed,
For nature's jokes are truly the best!

So gather round, let's share some grins,
In this woodland where laughter begins.
With every giggle, a new tale spins,
And joy is found among furry fins.

Rhyme in the Stalks and Leaves

In a patch where the grasses tickle your toes,
A family of frogs wear their finest clothes.
They croak out tunes, everyone knows,
While fireflies flash, a dance that glows.

Ants march in line, a parade on repeat,
Carrying crumbs, oh what a great feat!
They boast as they move, so quick on their feet,
While the butterflies tease with a flutter and beat.

Grasshoppers leap with a spring and a hop,
Making friends with the bugs who can't stop.
They sing 'till the sun meets the evening stop,
This little concert just won't ever drop!

So join in the fun, no need for a plan,
In this whimsical world, be quick if you can.
Laughter is found in a quirky good clan,
Where nature's fun is for every girl and man.

Echoes of Nature's Rhythm

With each gust of wind comes a giggly sound,
The fluttering leaves, a dance profound.
Twigs snap like jokes that bounce all around,
While the chipmunks' chatter is truly unbound.

A porcupine winks, and a fox plays the fool,
Make sure not to miss this grand woodland school.
With laughs in the air, who needs a pool?
When nature brings laughter, we all play the tool.

The crickets compose symphonies at dusk,
While the moonlight shines on this wonder, so husk.
Each echo of nature, a whimsical musk,
We jam to the chorus of laughter and rust.

So sway with the trees, let the fun take its toll,
Every rustle and twirl makes the evening a stroll.
Join in the laughter, let your heart feel whole,
In the rhythm of nature, find joy in the roll.

The Woven Tapestry of Green

In a quilt made of leaves where the sunlight plays,
Lively critters dance in a leafy ballet.
The shadows chuckle, making mischief all day,
As laughter weaves through the branches that sway.

The spiders spin webs that twinkle like stars,
While beetles parade in their miniature cars.
The chorus of nature knows no real bars,
Each giggle and grin becomes part of the jars.

A snail tells a tale that unfolds so slow,
While much faster friends giggle, 'What do you know?'
Each moment a movie that puts on a show,
Where nature's odd antics put smiles on the row.

So let's share some giggles beneath this green dome,
In the wild wonders where we find our home.
Every flutter and chirp invites us to roam,
In laughter and joy, we are never alone.

The Ballad of the Swaying Hollows

In the hollow where the tall stalks sway,
A frog popped out to start his play.
He tripped on roots, what a funny sight,
He croaked a tune, dancing in delight.

Squirrels joined in, with acorn hats,
While sparrows chirped and wiggled their flats.
A dance-off broke, the champion's crown,
Was won by a snail, who moved so slow and brown.

The wind took jests, tickling each face,
With whispers of laughter in this green place.
The sun peeked through, a cheeky grin,
As the whole hollow rocked, filled with kin.

So when you hear a rustle and cheer,
Know the hollows are laughing, loud and clear.
Join in the fun, don't let it pass,
For nature's a stage, and life's a class.

Enchantment in the Rustic Grove

In the rustic grove, where friends convene,
A critter parade, the funniest scene.
A rabbit with shades, sipping in style,
While a tortoise twerks, oh what a smile!

The bloom of the flowers, they giggle in hues,
As bees breakdance, unfazed by the blues.
A goat on a tightrope, with wobbling flair,
Each tip and each twirl, a comedic affair.

The leaves roll their eyes, and the branches shake,
At the antics displayed, for goodness' sake!
A squirrel tried limbo, fell flat on its face,
Yet bounced right back, now that's some grace!

So if you wander to this joyful place,
Expect laughter and fun; it's a riotous space.
Join the grove's antics, let giggles ignite,
In this woodland wonder, it feels just right.

The Duet of Leaf and Light

In a dance of shadows, where sunlight plays,
Leaves crack up at the frog's silly ways.
A cricket recites a joke under a tree,
While sunbeams chuckle, laughing with glee.

The breeze rolls in, with a playful breeze,
Tickling the flowers, a ticklish tease.
A butterfly dancer, twirling about,
Got tangled in webs, oh what a clout!

But laughter is magic in this bright scene,
As the forest chuckles, keeps spirits keen.
A lizard in shades, strikes a smooth pose,
Declares he's the coolest—everybody knows!

So harmonize here with the leaf and light,
Join in the laughter, let joy take flight.
In this duet, let your giggles resound,
For a world filled with humor is truly profound.

Soft Serenades from the Deep Woods

In the deep woods where the shadows lurk,
Animals gather, for a humorous perk.
A raccoon strums a lute made of bark,
Sings of adventures, with a funny remark.

The owl's wisdom, mixed with a wink,
Sparks candid giggles, oh how they think!
A hedgehog with glasses, recites a tall tale,
About a lost shoe, on an epic scale.

Fireflies blink in rhythm and sync,
Joining the fun with a sparkle and wink.
The groundhog bursts forth, in a dramatic flair,
Announcing the party, with flair beyond compare!

So wander through woods, let laughter ensue,
With serenades soft, creating a brew.
In the embrace of trees, where joy gently bends,
Find humor in nature, where laughter transcends.

Tales from the Enchanted Grove

In the grove where laughter sings,
A raccoon wears a crown of rings.
He juggles nuts with such delight,
While fireflies dance, oh what a sight!

The squirrels gossip, tails all a-swish,
About the raccoon's giant fish.
But really it's just his lunch, you see,
He claims it's magic, like a wizard's spree!

Magic beans with legs run amok,
They go around, quacking like a duck.
The owls hoot jokes and roll their eyes,
While frogs wear hats as the sun starts to rise!

So if you wander through this place,
Don't take the stories at face.
For in this grove where fun is rife,
The silly spins the wheel of life!

The Melody of Rustling Greens

In the rustling leaves, a song breaks free,
A chorus of crickets and buzzing bees.
A caterpillar dances, wiggling its rear,
With dreams of someday being a deer!

The parrot squawks, a bard of the trees,
Filling the air with puns and tease.
"I'm the best singer, no croak can compare,
Just look at my feathers, beyond all compare!"

Then a hedgehog chimes in, rolling around,
With snappy remarks that astound and confound.
"I'll play you a tune from my prickly shell,
But watch your step, it may not end well!"

So join in the laughter and share in the cheer,
As nature's own band makes all things clear.
In this grove of giggles, sunlight gleams,
Life's a fantastic collection of dreams!

Rhapsody of the Elongated Stems

Among tall greens that sway and sway,
The rabbits hold a dance ballet.
With tangled feet in a comic mess,
They hop and twirl, then laugh no less!

"Who knew we could dance?" one bunny exclaimed,
As he tripped and fell, feeling quite ashamed.
"Pick me up!" he cried with a big floppy flop,
They all giggled loud, then started to hop!

A grasshopper judge with a tiny gavel,
Declared them the best in a wiggly travel.
"Let's take a bow, no time to be meek,
For our hearts beat wild; let's go sneak a peek!"

The show must go on; they twirled on by,
While clouds chuckled softly up high in the sky.
The elongated stems sway to their beat,
An uproarious ensemble, oh what a treat!

Chronicles of the Verdant Wilderness

In the wilds where stories abound,
A turtle wears boots, exploring the ground.
"Look at me sprint!" he proudly brags,
While a snail nearby leisurely drags.

"Don't race, my friend, it's all quite the lark,
I'll reach the finish when the sun's gone dark!"
With a wink and a grin, he picks up the pace,
While the turtle chuckles, enjoying the chase.

A chorus of laughter from bushes nearby,
As chipmunks tumble, oh me, oh my!
"Let's form a band," they gleefully squeak,
"While the moon wears a smile on its glowing cheek!"

So gather around, let the tales unfold,
Of silly escapades and laughter bold.
In the verdant wild, where mischief doesn't cease,
Each day's an adventure, a fun-loving feast!

Harmony in Leaves and Wind

In the forest, leaves take flight,
Dancing silly in the light.
Whispers giggle through the trees,
Even branches join with ease.

A squirrel trips on a twig,
Laughs resound, it's quite a gig.
Twisting, turning, in a whirl,
Nature's stage, let chaos unfurl.

Sunbeams chuckle on the ground,
As shadows stretch, they twirl around.
Each gust carries a secret joke,
Where birds chirp in a funny cloak.

Together they sway, no grand plan,
Life's little wonders, just as they can.
With every rustle and every cheer,
The harmony of fun is always near.

Serenade of the Gilded Blades

Sharp as wit, the grasses sway,
Giggles echo, come what may.
Guided by a breeze so bold,
   Stories of the silly told.

A snail on a ride, oh what a sight!
Zooms past, giving us a fright.
Golden blades applaud with glee,
   While daisies join in jubilee.

Swaying side to side with grace,
They can't help but wear a face.
Every rustle, a playful tease,
   Tickling all, a merry breeze.

In this laughter, life is bright,
Every turn, a sheer delight.
Nature strums its whimsical tune,
With playful tales beneath the moon.

The Elegy of the Whispering Reeds

In a river, reeds stand tall,
Whispering secrets to us all.
They tell of frogs with lofty dreams,
Bartering jokes in moonlit beams.

A fish leaps high, a splash, a laugh,
While crickets join the aftermath.
Riptides play a funny game,
As reeds shake hands, the fish get fame.

Every breeze, a tickled sound,
Making waves, around and round.
Songs of the water, sweet and clear,
Make us grin from ear to ear.

In this elegy of fate,
The jokes of nature, they create.
With every sway and every cheer,
Life's finest humor, always near.

Songs from the Woodland Haven

In the woods, where shadows play,
Critters join in a funny fray.
Singing songs of joy and cheer,
From acorns bright, they craft a sphere.

A rabbit hops, a dance begins,
Brushing leaves like old-time sins.
With every thump, the forest wakes,
Carrying laughter in its makes.

Mice take a bow and cheese they share,
While owls hoot with clever flair.
Echoes twirl through trees so grand,
Creating joy, not just a band.

In every corner, smiles align,
Nature's jokes are so divine.
From woodland haven, tales ascend,
Final notes, where fun won't end.

The Calm Between the Leaves

In the shade where mischief hides,
Laughter dances, joy abides.
A squirrel slips on morning dew,
And every giggle feels brand new.

The tree branches gently sway,
As critters plot to steal the day.
A playful breeze begins to tease,
With rustling tones that aim to please.

A rabbit hops with silly flair,
While foxes plot with pouts and stares.
In leafy laughter, moments bind,
Creating tales of every kind.

Beneath the green, a joke takes flight,
With chirps and chuckles, pure delight.
In nature's jest, we find our pace,
In this grand, leafy, laughing space.

Silken Tones of the Thicket

With every rustle, secrets spill,
A frog leaps in with perfect skill.
It croaks a tune that makes us grin,
As butterflies embark, they spin.

A crabby hedgehog scolds the sun,
For waking him before his fun.
He rolls away with pointy pride,
In this jolly thicket, he will hide.

Chirping birds in discord sing,
With off-key notes, they're quite the thing.
Their melodies, a comic play,
That makes the harmony decay.

Whimsical whispers fill the air,
As chipmunks run without a care.
In nature's band, the laughter springs,
With silken tones and funny flings.

Chants of the Gentle Breeze

A breeze blows softly, tickling leaves,
While extra smoothness gives us heaves.
A babbling brook begins to chuckle,
As pebbles tease and puddles buckle.

Hiccups from a nearby brook,
Make frogs dive with startled looks.
Squirrels wobble, tails a-flap,
In the chaos, they misstep, zap!

The wind hums low, a playful tune,
As moths pose like a dancing loon.
With laughter woven through the night,
They twirl and swirl in pure delight.

In these winds, all troubles cease,
With whispers of unwarranted peace.
Together we share our giggly tease,
In the delightful, gentle breeze.

Treetop Dreams and Woodland Whispers

In treetops high, the dreams take flight,
As owls trade jokes beneath the night.
With wings spread wide, they hoot and tease,
In moonlit groves, they shimmy with ease.

A raccoon peeks through leafy seams,
In search of cookies, or so it deems.
With sticky paws, it snatches a treat,
And scampers off on light, furry feet.

The whispers weave through trunks and twigs,
As fireflies light their funny gigs.
They dance in patterns, bright and bold,
Crafting stories never told.

In this woodland, laughter swells,
With every critter sharing spells.
In treetop dreams and whispers so sly,
Together in humor, we will fly.

Lullabies of the Swaying Green

In the grove where the tall ones sway,
The wind hums tunes in a funny way.
Leaves laugh out loud and start to dance,
Even the squirrels join in the prance.

Critters converse in their own sweet chatter,
Giggling at shadows, what's the matter?
Each rustle and wiggle brings a grin,
Nature's comedy show, let's begin!

Even the crickets sing in delight,
Telling tales of a clumsy flight.
A twig tips over, then off it goes,
Nature's slapstick, oh how it shows!

So lay down your worries, join the spree,
In this leafy realm, wild and free.
With laughter abounding, joy won't cease,
Let's dance in the green, find our peace.

Sonnet of the Stillness

In quiet woods where the shades conspire,
A raccoon struts as if he's on fire.
He slips on leaves, oh what a sight,
His antics spark giggles, pure delight.

Whispers of branches in bated breath,
As owls hoot claims of sighting with heft.
But little do they know, with all that pride,
A skunk sneaks past, laughter's ally worldwide!

A turtle plods, caught in his own race,
While bees buzz by, with great eagerness.
Nature's misfits in a glorious folly,
In stillness, they bring forth the jolly.

So pause in the hush, let your heart chuckle,
For inside the calm, lies joy that'll snuggle.
With every whisper, the earth plays its tune,
In funny serenity, we're all immune.

Harmonies Beneath the Canopy

Underneath the leafy roof so grand,
Nestled soft, there's a zany band.
Frogs on drums and birds on the strings,
Creating a ruckus, oh how it sings!

Mice wear tuxedos, vowing to waltz,
While ants in a line practice their faults.
Every note floats, tickling the air,
Where laughter and music blend without care.

From root to branch, oh what a show,
With giggling sprites adding to the flow.
A tune that dances, invites us all,
Filling our hearts at nature's call.

So sway to the rhythm, let spirits fly,
In this forest dance, come, my oh my!
With each happy note, let us hum along,
In harmonies sweet, where we all belong.

Echoes from the Forest Floor

On the ground where the odd ones play,
Echoes of laughter skip on their way.
A worm tells a joke, it's quite the feat,
While beetles roll by on tiny feet.

Leaves crunch underfoot, a zany sound,
As shadows prance in joy all around.
A gopher peeks with a sly little smirk,
His antics, a highlight, in the dirt work.

A raccoon's caper, quite out of line,
Turning the earth into a big vine.
Funny things happen as daylight dims,
Nature's delight, as night starts to brim.

So wander the path where chuckles abound,
With each step you take, let joy be found.
In echoes of laughter that fill the night,
The forest's pure magic brings pure delight.

The Serenade Beneath the Starlit Canopy

Beneath the stars, we danced so free,
The squirrels joined in a jubilee.
A raccoon sang, his voice quite bold,
While owls hooted tales of old.

The fireflies blinked, a light parade,
As we played games the moonlight made.
A caterpillar slipped on glee,
And landed right upon my knee!

With every laugh, the shadows grew,
As crickets strummed a tune they knew.
The night wore on, so loose and bright,
While shadows twirled in sheer delight.

At dawn we snickered, dreams unfurled,
Recapping antics of our world.
In nature's arms, our giggles soared,
A silly song, forever adored.

The Tails of Tranquil Wilderness

In the woods where the forest plays,
A fox slipped in a clumsy daze.
He tripped on roots, then gave a snort,
Imitating a wild sport.

The rabbits cheered, their sides did ache,
As they wobbled for a theater shake.
Squirrels threw acorns like confetti,
While birds chirped back, an ode so petty.

A deer pranced in with a pompous air,
Challenging all with a gentle stare.
But slipped on grass, oh what a sight!
He laughed along, joined in their flight.

Together they roamed, a merry spree,
Celebrating nature's revelry.
In every tumble, every dive,
The laughter soared, the woods revived.

The Echoing Verse of Wind and Leaf

The wind whistled tunes through leafy tops,
While dandelions danced, doing hops.
A gust swept by, oh what a tease,
Tickling toes like the finest breeze.

The leaves clapped hands, a rustling cheer,
As we joined in, our voices clear.
"Whoosh!" went the sound of a little frog,
Jumping in rhythm, all in a fog.

A squirrel with flair, dressed up for the day,
Challenged the breeze to a playful fray.
He leaped and twirled, oh what a clown,
As the leaves whispered secrets, upside down.

Echoes of laughter filled the grove,
As nature's chorus, we all strove.
Each breeze a quip, each leaf a jest,
In this leafy realm, we were all blessed.

The Enchantment of Verdant Melodies

Among the greens where laughter blooms,
The flowers hummed in silly tunes.
A bumblebee wobbled and spun,
Claiming a flower, just for fun.

The sunbeams giggled, tossed shadows wide,
As toads croaked songs with cheeky pride.
"Leap!" said the frog, with a playful croak,
Jumping right onto a startled oak.

The daisies twirled, a bright ballet,
When a squirrel skipped with a grand display.
In every nook, there was a surprise,
Where critters plotted and shared their guise.

As twilight came, the melody swayed,
In nature's magic, the fun portrayed.
Together we sang, till stars glowed bright,
In our verdant stage, pure delight.

The Story of the Whistling Leaves

In the grove where leaves do sway,
A squirrel sings without delay.
He thinks he's quite the melody,
But birds just stare in quiet glee.

A rabbit hops, a tune he hums,
While ants march on without the drums.
The breeze takes flight, a playful tease,
And rustles through the laughing trees.

Harmonies in the Shade of Giants

Beneath the great and towering stalks,
The critters gather, swap their talks.
A frog croaks out a stumpy beat,
While crickets chirp with tiny feet.

A raccoon jives with flashy moves,
As ladybugs find their own grooves.
Each note, a tale of silly rhyme,
In the shade, they dance with time.

Tales from Whispering Hollows

In hollowed depths where shadows play,
A wise old owl has much to say.
He hoots a tale of fishy schemes,
Of sneaky fish in watery dreams.

With giggles shared among the crew,
The badger joins, with tales anew.
A fox howls at the moonlit glow,
And all join in, their laughter flows.

The Whispered Legends of the Blades

Among the stalks, the secrets spill,
Of grass blades bending at their will.
A dandelion with silly hair,
Claims he's a lion, fierce and rare.

With giggling whispers, the wind complies,
As butterflies dance beneath the skies.
Each legend spun with a playful twist,
In daylight's glow, they can't resist.

The Vocalization of the Emerald Shadows

In the green shadows, critters sing,
A frog dressed in tweed, what a strange thing!
He hops with flair, a top hat askew,
While ants in tuxedos dance on cue.

The trees clap their branches, join in the fun,
Squirrels chuckle loudly, 'Oh, what a pun!'
With laughter so bright, the night takes a bow,
While fireflies twinkle, saying, 'Look at us now!'

An owl wearing glasses reads jokes from a book,
While beetles do stand-up in every nook.
The shadows all giggle, the leaves sway with glee,
In this wild concert, we're all VIP!

So come join the echo where giggles reside,
In a world made of whispers, where joy likes to hide.
With every funny tale and silly charade,
The emerald shadows will laugh till they fade.

The Narrative of the Woodland Serenade

Once a squirrel thought it clever to dance,
He slipped on a nut—what a ridiculance!
The birds in the trees all cackled so loud,
As he spun like a top, in front of the crowd.

A rabbit, quite dapper in a coat and tie,
Told tales of his love for a sweet pumpkin pie.
While frogs croaked their own version of blues,
'Ribbit while you can, we've got nothing to lose!'

The beetles held backstage, took bets on the score,
'Will he land on his feet or go face-first on the floor?'
But the forest kept jiving, with all of its grace,
As laughter and music twirled in the space.

So gather round, friends, hear the woodland song,
Where every misstep can't be wrong for long.
With giggles and wiggles, life's joys are displayed,
In the love of mischief, the serenade played.

The Aesthetic Grace of the Glades

In the glades where the critters all prance with delight,
A raccoon in a tutu stole every spotlight.
He twirled on the grass, with some twigs in his hair,
While the sun spilled gold, spreading joy everywhere.

The rabbits held acorns, like microphones tight,
Rapping their rhythms, dancing under moonlight.
The owls cheered them on, with a hoot and a wink,
Their feathers a-fluffing, they joined in the stink.

With tapestries woven from laughter and cheer,
Each brush of the wind made the fun crystal clear.
Pine trees lined up, like fans yelling 'Bravo!'
As the raccoon took bows with a huge, goofy glow.

So if you could wander where giggles abound,
Let the glades be your stage, let your joy be unbound.
For in this sweet haven where silliness blooms,
Life's whimsical tales chase away all the glooms.

The Chants of Quiet Resilience

Under whispers of leaves, the critters convene,
A turtle tries yoga, but he's stuck in between.
He chants out his mantras, with a snort and a sigh,
While a lizard does backflips, oh my, oh my!

The quiet ones giggle, their voices a hum,
As they cheer for the turtle, 'You'll soon find your sum!'
With a wiggle and jiggle, he gives it a shot,
But falls on his shell, 'Hey, what's the big plot?'

The wise old owl hoots, 'Life's fun, don't you see?
It's the flaws that bring smiles, just let it be free!'
While crickets provide a soundtrack so neat,
As the laughter and stories bring light to the heat.

So celebrate quirks in this wild little place,
Where resilience wears laughter, with humor and grace.
And when days feel heavy, just look for the cheer,
In the chants of the quiet, you'll find it is near.

Ballad of the Gentle Thicket

In a grove where laughter leaps,
A squirrel in a top hat beeps.
He lost his way, oh what a sight,
Chasing shadows in the night.

A dancing leaf, it tickles him right,
Wobbling and twirling, a silly flight.
The breeze joins in with a playful tease,
'Tis a frolicsome world, filled with gleeful ease.

With pranks and giggles, the critters play,
As whispers of the wind drift away.
A frog croaks loudly, "Where's the fun?
I'd trade my fly for a side of bun!"

And so they sway, each critter finds,
Joy in the thicket where mirth unwinds.
With a wink and a nod, the world's a jest,
In this gentle thicket, they find their best.

Rhythms of the Evergreen Spires

In the spires, a party takes flight,
Two owls in tuxedos, oh what a sight!
They hoot and they holler, dance on a branch,
Stirring the leaves for a whimsical chance.

A hedgehog twirls in a clumsy spin,
With every misstep, the laughter begins.
Squirrels in bowties throw acorns around,
Competing for best at their leafy ground.

The rhythm is wild, the beats are loud,
The shadows jump, oh, they're so proud!
They march and they prance, a motley crew,
In the evergreen spires, the fun just grew.

As twilight sets in, the party's still bright,
An echo of joy lit by starlight.
With twinks and giggles, they dance 'til dawn,
In the rhythm of life, merriment's drawn.

Voices Amongst the Canes

Among the canes, a ruckus is heard,
A parrot's squawk steals the scene, absurd!
With tales of pineapple and drunken bees,
He charms the crowd with his gossip and tease.

The frogs join in with their playful croaks,
Attempting punchlines, oh, what a hoax!
A turtle slides in with a slow-paced joke,
"We're all in a hurry, but none of us smoke!"

From whispers to roars, the humor spreads wide,
With canes as their stage, they laugh and collide.
A ladybug winks, "Let's start a band!
I'll play the leaf, you take the sand."

So in the canes, while the sunlight fades,
Voices arise in jubilant cascades.
Sharing their stories, with chuckles and cheer,
Their moments of friendship, forever held dear.

The Anthem of Swaying Shadows

In the shadows, a riddle unfolds,
A raccoon declares, "I've got treasures untold!"
He pulls out an acorn, a shiny old key,
"We'll unlock the funniest things you will see!"

The shadows sway under the moon's playful glance,
Each twirl bringing giggles, a whimsical dance.
With whispers of mischief, the breeze can't stay still,
Unraveling secrets, just waiting to thrill.

A hare hops in wearing mismatched shoes,
"I slip and I slide, but I still refuse!"
He tumbles and rolls amidst the night mist,
For any slight stumble is too hard to resist.

And just like that, the shadows have sung,
With laughter and joy, hearts forever young.
The anthem plays on, till the break of the day,
In the sway of the shadows, they dance and they play.

Symphony of the Verdant Canopy

In the forest, oh what a sight,
Leaves are dancing, feeling quite light.
A squirrel's mischief, a comic's play,
He steals my sandwich, then scurries away.

The raccoons gather for a late-night feast,
They tiptoe around, not wanting to be ceased.
With laughter echoing through the trees,
They mess with my hat, oh how they tease!

In the shadows, a wise old owl,
He hoots with humor, oh what a prowl!
Tales of birdseed, the quirkiest meal,
Every fluff and feather, a tickling reel.

As the day fades, the stars all wink,
A porcupine's dance makes the critters think.
Nature's orchestra, a comedic score,
In the canopy, I'm never a bore.

The Legacy of the Lush Forest

Leaves whisper secrets, so full of glee,
A parrot squawks, 'Come look at me!'
He mimics my laugh, it's quite the show,
I can't help but giggle; the forest's glow.

A turtle sneezes, what a big sound,
Frogs leap around; they're joyfully bound.
The bee in a bonnet, buzzing with pride,
Trips on a petal, oops! What a ride!

The trees tell stories with creaks and groans,
Of critters who dance on their lush green thrones.
Their roots intertwined, sharing a joke,
Life in their shade, a funny little poke.

As daylight fades, the glowworms come,
They twinkle and shine, but they're far from dumb.
With a flicker and flash, they pull a prank,
In this lush legacy, nothing's too dank.

The Poetry of Gentle Breezes

Oh how the breeze whispers soft and sweet,
It tickles the daisies at my wandering feet.
A wind that sings with a playful tune,
Fluttering leaves, dancing under the moon.

A butterfly flirts, so bold and bright,
She tells the grass, 'Let's take to flight!'
But a gust comes in, she's caught in the fray,
Off she goes, in a whimsical way.

The daisies giggle, the daisies sway,
'We'll never let go, just come what may!'
But when the breeze swirls, they squeal in delight,
Swirling and twirling, oh what a sight!

In the heart of the meadow, laughter will rise,
For even the wind has its funny sides.
With each gentle whisper, a chuckle breaks free,
Nature's own humor, wild as can be.

Awakening the Silent Grove

In the quiet grove, there's a rustle of mirth,
A critter pokes through, pollinating the earth.
Frogs croak in chorus, it's a giddy tune,
A raccoon juggles nuts, oh, what a buffoon!

The mushrooms chuckle, all dressed in green,
Their tops like hats, a delightful scene.
A snail takes a peek and joins in the fun,
'Slow and steady wins,' he says with a pun.

A breeze swoops in, carrying laughs,
It teases the branches, and no one dares crash.
The trees start to sway, a green fashion show,
In their leafy attire, they steal the show!

As shadows lengthen, the night takes its hold,
A chorus of crickets, funny stories are told.
In this silent grove, our spirits do soar,
With laughter and joy, forever more.

Whispers in the Tall Grasses

The grasses laugh as they sway,
A ticklish breeze holds court today.
A cricket sings its silly tune,
While frogs croak loud, invoking a moon.

A tumbleweed does a wobbly dance,
In this grassland, all take a chance.
The sun dips down, it twirls and spins,
As nature's show of silliness begins.

Bouncing bugs wear tiny hats,
While playful mice perform with rats.
Each leaf a gaffe, each rustle a jest,
In the grassy realm, we all are blessed!

So come and join the merry quick,
Dance with the grass; life's a fun trick.
In whispers low, the laughter grows,
In the tall grasses, anything goes!

Dancer of the Wind

The wind does a jig, with hops and skips,
It twirls around like a dancer flips.
With every whoosh, it plays a prank,
Tipping the hats of all at the bank.

Leaves pirouette in a grand ballet,
While birds chuckle at the feathery play.
A squirrel slips on an acorn's shell,
And with a flip, it gives a yell!

The sun chuckles, it rolls on the ground,
As shadows stretch, fun is all around.
With giggles and gales, the world spins free,
The wind is the star, come dance with me!

Oh, join the breeze, let laughter sway,
In nature's shuffle, we'll find our way.
A spiral of joy on the winds does sing,
In this raucous realm, let the laughter ring!

Shadows of the Forest Grove

The shadows jive beneath the trees,
Tickling roots with every breeze.
A mischievous owl hoots with glee,
As shadows dance, wild and free.

The squirrels chuckle, swapping tales,
Of epic leaps and funny fails.
Mice play hide and seek in the dark,
While raccoons plot tricks with a spark.

In the glade, where laughter's loud,
The trees sway with a giggling crowd.
A hedgehog rolls down a slope with pride,
As shadows laugh, they can't help but hide!

Join the fun 'neath the leafy dome,
In this shadowy world, we can roam.
Each whispered joke, a joyous groove,
In the forest grove, let's all approve!

Green Echoes and Silent Songs

Green echoes swell in the afternoon,
A soft rustle breaks the afternoon.
A grasshopper strums on a leafy string,
The forest hums, let the laughter ring!

With whispers bright, the ferns confide,
In secret tales where giggles hide.
A lizard slides down a sunlit shard,
While worms wiggle in a funny yard.

Through the leaves flows a gentle tease,
As whispers duck and dart with ease.
Every sound, a comic giggle,
In green echoes, we all wiggle!

So gather round, let joy unfold,
With silent songs that never grow old.
In this verdant choir, we take our stand,
As laughter sprouts from the soft green land!

The Muse of the Grove

In the grove, where giggles play,
The trees perform a wobbly sway.
Squirrels wear their acorn hats,
And dance like tiny acrobats.

The sunbeams slip through leafy lace,
Tickling all in this joyful space.
A robin sings a silly tune,
As frogs leap by in a mock cartoon.

Butterflies flaunt their vibrant dress,
While bees just bumble, causing a mess.
Here laughter flows as rivers do,
In a whimsical world where wonders brew.

So swing your arms, let worries flee,
Join the nature's absurd comedy.
A nudge from a branch, a giggle so bright,
In the grove, everything feels just right!

Reflections in the Green Mirage

In a pond, a frog hops proud,
Wearing a crown that's made of cloud.
The fish beneath with laughter bubble,
At the frog's leap and watery trouble.

The sky reflects in shades of green,
Where dragonflies twirl like stars unseen.
A turtle grins with a wink so sly,
Pretending to be the next sky-high fly.

Ripples giggle with each splash made,
Secrets shared in this leafy glade.
The breeze tickles the reeds just so,
While willows sway with a graceful flow.

Life's a mirror, full of jest,
Where nature's whims are at their best.
So join the fray, don't be shy,
Laugh with the forest as time floats by!

Secrets of the Whispering Woodlands

In the woodlands, whispers play,
Trees confess secrets in breezy sway.
A raccoon with a mask of charm,
Sneaks by, but means no harm.

The moss giggles underfoot,
As rabbits hop and hoot and hoot.
A trail of nuts and seeds spills wide,
All hoping for a playful ride.

Nature's humor, a daily show,
With ticklish petals that dance to and fro.
The wind carries jokes from afar,
As fireflies twinkle like tiny stars.

So stroll through this woodland bliss,
Awaiting giggles you can't miss.
For every tree has a tale to share,
In the secrets of a world so rare!

Enchanted by Nature's Breath

Under the sun, the flowers prance,
In a quirky and colorful dance.
Bees wear hats made of dew,
And zoom around just for you.

A playful breeze, a jolly sigh,
Carries laughter through the sky.
The daisies chuckle, petals wide,
As ants parade, filled with pride.

The tall grass sways, a bustling throng,
Nature humming a silly song.
Clouds drift by, dressed up in white,
Throwing shapes that bring delight.

So take a breath in nature's glow,
Join the laughter, let your worries go.
For in this realm, fun finds its way,
As we celebrate each cheerful day!

The Reverie of Shimmering Dusk

In twilight's glow, a dance begins,
With crickets chirping silly sins,
A frog jumps high, a leap so bold,
While nearby, a cat slips on the cold.

A firefly flickers, doing a jig,
While a raccoon wears a humorous wig,
The sun bids adieu with a chuckle and grin,
As twilight whispers, 'Come on in!'

The stars appear, a mischievous crowd,
They wink and laugh, all feeling proud,
'Look at the moon, dressed in cheese,
Even the night knows how to tease!'

In dreams we tumble, a jolly spree,
With laughter echoing, carefree and free,
Under shimmering skies, oh what a sight,
The world's just a stage, in the fading light.

Glistening Sagas of the Woodland

In the forest's heart, a tale unfolds,
With squirrels chattering as the sun beholds,
A raccoon capers, searching for treats,
While owls hoot jokes, with rhythm in beats.

The brook bubbles over, giggling away,
'Catch me if you can!' it seems to say,
A deer prances with a spring in its step,
With flowers in its antlers, a quirky prep.

The mushrooms converse, with hats all abloom,
Sharing secrets beneath the moon's plume,
'The world's a circus, so join the fun,
Every twig and leaf, a story begun!'

As daylight fades, the creatures align,
Under twinkling stars, they dine and recline,
A woodland party, oh such delight,
Where laughter echoes through the night.

The Cadence of Tall Shadows

In shadows that stretch as the day bows low,
Tall figures waltz, putting on a show,
A squirrel tiptoes, adorned with charms,
While the tall trees sway, with open arms.

A whisper of mischief rides the night,
As shadows chuckle, feeling just right,
'Oh look at that spider, spinning a tale,
While the moon just giggles, without fail!'

Laughter erupts from the breeze so light,
As fireflies twirl, stealing the night,
In this joyful dance of shadow and beam,
Life's just a jest, or so it would seem!

As stars paint the sky with a twinkling grid,
The world smiles softly, no reason to hid,
In the cadence of tales, we find our claim,
With joyous shadows, we play the game.

The Poetic Breeze Amongst the Greens

A gentle breeze whispers through the trees,
With rustling leaves tickling, oh such a tease,
A chicken dances, flapping its wings,
While the grass giggles at the joy it brings.

The daisies shout, 'Let's have some fun!'
As the sun peeks in, saying, 'I'm not done!',
A rabbit hops, with a hat on its head,
Spinning around, in its own little thread.

With butterflies fluttering, and bees on a spree,
Offering honeyed laughs, sweet as can be,
The garden's alive with a whimsical rhyme,
Every blade of grass joins in the time!

As dusk sways softly, with a wink and a hum,
Life's full of laughter, a jubilant drum,
In this merry concerto of chirps and sways,
The breeze whispers secrets of sunny days.